God's Word for God's Children

The Garden of Eden

by Olin Edward James

Copyright © 2015
First edition published 2015
All rights reserved. No part of this book may be reproduced, stored in a retrieval system, or transmitted in any form or by any means – electronic, mechanical, photocopying, recording, or otherwise, without written permission from the publisher.
Illustrator: Jess Wadland
Author Family Photo: Esther Abel
Editor: Sharon Spencer

Printed in the United States of America
Aneko Press – Our Readers Matter™
www.anekopress.com
Aneko Press, Life Sentence Publishing, and our logos are trademarks of
Life Sentence Publishing, Inc.
203 E. Birch Street
P.O. Box 652
Abbotsford, WI 54405
RELIGION / Christian Life / Family
Paperback ISBN: 978-1-62245-191-3
Ebook ISBN: 978-1-62245-192-0
10   9   8   7   6   5   4   3   2   1
Available where books are sold.

About the Author

The author, raised by Godly parents, is from a small Ohio town. He is married to his wonderful wife, Christy, and has two incredible daughters, Hannah Katherine and Gwenyth Irene (thus the KathIrene Kids). He has studied God's word in Ohio, New York, and Alberta, Canada, and desires that all would read and love the Scriptures, abide in Jesus, walk in the Spirit, and glorify God.

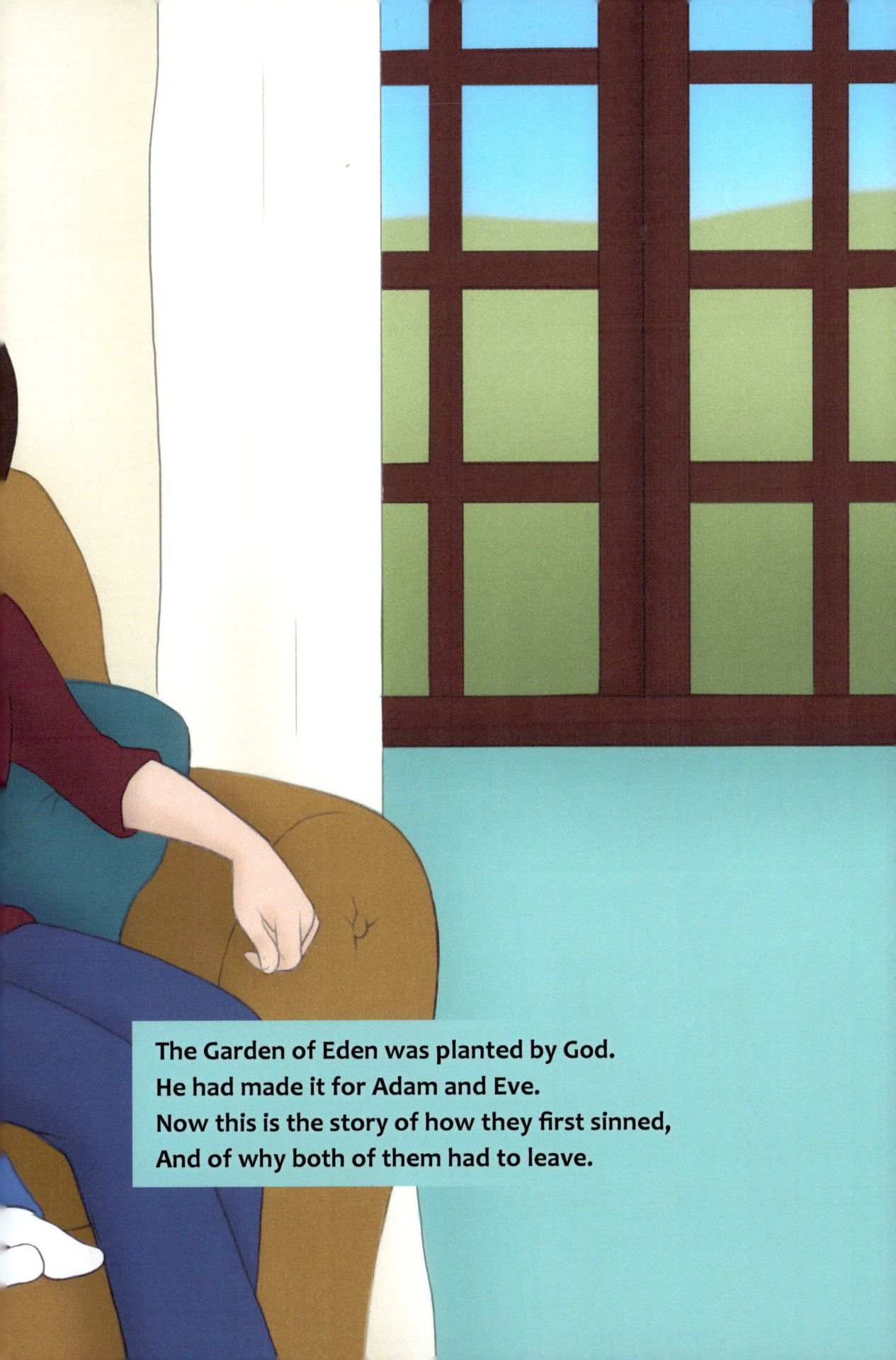

The Garden of Eden was planted by God.
He had made it for Adam and Eve.
Now this is the story of how they first sinned,
And of why both of them had to leave.

Adam and Eve, they had never yet sinned,
And God gave them one simple command:
"From the tree of the knowledge of good and evil,
Don't eat, but enjoy all the rest of the land."

Satan appeared in the form of a snake,
And asked Eve, "Did God mean what He said?"
"God told us," said Eve, "If we eat of that tree,
We will certainly both end up dead."

"God was just saying that, Eve," said the snake.
"For surely that could not be true.
Here then is my theory of what will occur,
Of what eating that fruit now will do."

"Your eyes will be opened. You'll be just like God,
And you'll know good and evil," he said.
"Eve, listen to me. God made all those things up;
For I'm sure you will not end up dead."

Eve looked at the fruit of the tree; it looked good.
Would it really cause death as God told her it would?
What if instead it would open her eyes?
Eve ignored God and believed Satan's lies.

They had sinned against God. They had done what was wrong.
They now realized that Satan had lied!
God was coming to see them, and they were afraid!
What could they do now? They would hide!

God called out to them, for He knew where they were.
He asked, "Why are you hiding, you two?
Did you disobey Me? Did you eat from the tree?
Did you do what I said not to do?"

"The woman You made for me gave me the fruit,"
Said Adam to God, "So I ate."
"The serpent deceived me," Eve said to the Lord.
"Satan told me the fruit would be great!"

To the woman, God said, "Here's your punishment, Eve;
For you disobeyed Me, it is true.
You will now have great pain giving birth to a child,
And your husband will rule over you."

To Adam, God said,
"You have sinned against Me.
For you listened to Eve,
And you ate from that tree."

"So now you must work by the sweat of your brow,
With thistles and thorns all around.
Created you were from the dust of the earth;
You will die and return to the ground."

The Lord made them clothes from some animal skins,
That Adam and Eve could now wear.
Then God sent them out of the garden He'd made.
They were never allowed back in there.

No matter what anyone else says to you,
You can trust in God's word; it will always be true.
The Lord never lies, never leads us astray.
So follow God fully; it is the best way.

www.ingramcontent.com/pod-product-compliance
Lightning Source LLC
Chambersburg PA
CBHW041122070526
44584CB00002B/253